ALSO BY PETER GIZZI

Now It's Dark

Sky Burial: New and Selected Poems

Archeophonics

In Defense of Nothing: Selected Poems, 1987–2011

Threshold Songs

The Outernationale

Some Values of Landscape and Weather

Artificial Heart

Periplum and other poems

Fierce Elegy

Fierce Elegy

PETER GIZZI

WESLEYAN UNIVERSITY PRESS • MIDDLETOWN, CONNECTICUT

Wesleyan Poetry

Wesleyan University Press
Middletown CT 06459
www.wesleyan.edu/wespress

Hardcover ISBN 978-0-8195-0067-0
Paperback ISBN 978-0-8195-0068-7
Ebook ISBN 978-0-8195-0069-4

Library of Congress Cataloging-in Publication
Data appear at the back of the book.

5 4 3 2 1

CONTENTS

☆

for Suzanna Tamminen

all these years

Only in connection with a body
does a shadow make sense.

ROSMARIE WALDROP

Fierce Elegy

Findspot Unknown

Thus far we have spoken

only the codes,

a litany of survival.

Thus spoke the silvered asphodel

next to the factory ruin.

Sound carries on water.

My subject is the wind.

To take umbrage at what a tree can do,

watching one single birch

become lightning stunning the sky.

Landscape is a made thing,

to see the mind seeing itself.

To see thought, a wing

in night, the long brooding.

Take it, listen, the night is orchestral

when the power's on.

Everything disporting.

A furred wand upon nothingness.

I get it, it was good to leave the world,
to find myself in thou.
There's a lot to be said
for seeing in the dark,
and more to the light
when there's nothing to see.
If I write about the moon,
it's because it's there.
I am landlocked, surrounded
by rivers and lakes, pills and leaves.
I saw a better life, it was far off,
sun on moss next to a friend,
the softening air, the dandelion fluff.
It was kinda real, and kinda not.
Can't see it today.

And out of nothing, breath.
A beast-like shadow in the glass.
If I brought back every feeling I had
where would I put them,
what could they mean
to this world on the floor?

It was best to let the moon unravel

and focus the truth of the music.

It was best to let the music

unravel and focus the truth of night.

Like when I found you

in the back of my mind.

I am talking about people

and the night.

People inside the night.

The night and what we are made of.

The things and the people.

The signal and its noise.

I'm Good to Ghost

It was all so Orfeo
the other night.
When the face you carry
is not your own
and the history in this
is a history of
haunted ground.
The world is a veil.
Its effects total
the imagination.
What have I been doing
without me
all this time?
Don't know if
I want to anymore.
I wonder distance
and its discontents.
I trouble distance
nevertheless.

The poet is abuzz.

The poet becomes

a bug in air.

How did I lose you

between the rug

on my floor and

the sun setting

out the window,

between the radiator

and a dusky

kaleidoscopic light?

To wander that light

ingenious before dark.

To wonder the beautiful

so close to death.

Where do you go

when I don't see you?

Or who am I when

you're not around?

Revisionary

I've decided to let my inner weather out.
Even in the nerves flashing, some things
    are only shadow.
What's up with that?
My muse bruises me.
Some days I sit hours to be relieved
    by a word.
Today's word is invisible.

I'm putting trouble into place, turning
    toward what is.
Listening to stone translate into silence.
Here is an old rock covered with lichen
    in the mossy forest inside the self.
I like it here when it's green.
This is me evolving.
I'm hanging on. A whisper.
Certain prayers are tied to this ribbon.

How in hell can nature throw clay into art
    into a speaking being into air.
I saw a world that was an afternoon.
This cloud in my hand.
Sky pouring into sky reflecting the absolute
    of the lake.
The flock and its tangle of shadow.

Nearing the end, I could hear a lark.
Its trill fixing itself to my brain.
It seemed a thing becoming a wave.
A thing dissolving into the world
    as I found it.
Illegible. Agrammatical.
To parse the velocity of trusses and stars
    flowering here at the edge.
Calling me.

Dissociadelic

To be a desperate player
in the invisible world.
This is something different.
To have crossed over into ink
and to loiter and bleed out
on the occasion of the universe.
I've learned this.
My spirit broke long ago
so I won't be broken.
This is something quite different
inside the song.
Blurs. Gestures. Something loved.
Come as you are, collapsing
and thriving with endings
like beginnings.
When 8 Ball says "ask again."
When the day reveals
the prismatic systems of loss,

a blinding shimmer

on new blacktop in a sun shower.

Everything always in black.

Black wax. Black dress. Black hole.

Whatever.

When you're brought to your knees,

sing a song of praise.

When you're gutted,

embrace the whorl. FTW.

There's nothing like it.

Creeley Song

all that is lovely

in words, even

if gone to pieces

all that is lovely

gone, all of it

for love and

autobiography

as if I were

writing this

hello, listen

the plan is

the body and

all of it for love

now in pieces

all that is lovely

echoes still

in life & death

still memory

gardens open

onto windows

lovely, the charm

that mirrors

all that was, all

that is, lovely

in a song

Notes on Sound
and Vision

The consequence

of flesh also

comes into the painting.

The attitude of landscape

escapes into a body

thinking of the body.

The dark octave unsettled.

How far can vision

take one, how far

do we see

into the painting

thinking of painting,

thinking of canvas,

or the hand

that shaped the arc

loving distance?

Or the shape of

the human and the shape

of sleep and its dim shore,

its shadow sand,

marshland and a road.

Sometimes it's hard

to know the outline

of a body, there's

so many people inside.

So much room

for love and mayhem.

For now, come close,

come closer, come

into the reeds.

Come into

the intimate distance

of the picture field.

So much room

for death and song.

Come into the room

where the viewer

is the viewed.

When the thing itself

becomes the thing itself.

There are so

many people here.

Notre Musique

it's amazing anyone survives, an index cannot be simplified,
the dust stands up in time, moves with wind, wind off a
book closing, our music, men marching, murder-making,
movie marching, minor chords clang in this reel, meaning
the people of the book, shot, counter-shot, tanks rock over
hills and crush flora, jets rocket off the cruiser's vast deck,
all this formal collapse, forward-ho, war the constant, we
the variant, sonic trespass of the mind, our music disturbs
notes fingered on the keys' slight sustain, soloing in air,
yes, they all died very young

The Posthumous Life
of Childhood

The sun

in the chest

like a spell,

like folly,

wept I

and when

soot turns

to gravel

in the mind,

revealing a bad

morning light,

then am I

a refinery flame,

a cylinder,

a payload

unto nigh.

I'm cold,

boundless.

A clinical

darkness

grips the voice.

The wind

drives snow,

the I remains

frozen,

lashed,

the ruins of

anything.

To be in time,

this theater feeling,

but I forgot

the line,

seized,

limited by

the hour,

I saw that

emptiness,

my body,

that inner star.

I Am Who Sent Me

To have died in youth and remain.
To be good with that.

To forget now who was speaking.
Someone was always speaking.

To be in the yesterday of today,
lost in the morning's psychotropic green.

But the verb is to be, to be vigilant
and hungry across time

along with the words "I love"
blinking in the face of it.

Look for faces and you find
them everywhere.

That leafy Elm becoming a mouth.
Overhead, voices angular and taut

rebound in space
with an antique question.

Where are you now?
Now only words for lost things.

Language marching into empire,
starving the words.

Light throwing rhythmic shadows,
doppler and strange. Where are you?

Things for last things.
Still, at this almost moment

a voice to come as sunrise
and remember the mother.

And the father everywhere
inside migrating birds.

So brief, so gone.
This was the legacy of dew:

to learn these origins
as the origin of water.

Unguarded, you wake
and open into your face.

Freestyle. Fathomless.
To see that far into oneself

with only a tear for a mirror.
The shape of it.

I keep it close
as a shield against time.

Nimbus

in this hand

a chromosome

the mystery

of the ordinary

becoming

the me in I

a rosary

ready to turn

a hunger

for real things

like a wave

to salute

the real

when twilight

comes on

breathe in

breathe out

an archetype

calling to it

the earth

in orange light

a regalia

of lost music

no more

alive than me

this is not

a small poem

everything

in starlight

thin snow

fragile and

dream-lapsed

warped by wind

or anything

made of waves

like my body

and the rest

of the day

Monday

and April

pierced

like an echo

outlasting me

as if nothing

could polish

the sky

where the present

and phantom touch

where mirrors etc.

turn like weather

it's so random

becoming a self

the secret

to my own

piece of sky

behaving as

clouds do

another day

a macular blue

white, steel

a swatch of green

the afternoon

reflected green

wavy, transparent

and shadows

turn nothing

to nothingness

enter the O

in breath

an antiquity

of thought

a notebook opens

there are windows

in the notebook

and a road

birds, houses

trees, etc.

hunger

for the word

flower

where bees

work the bell

it is the I

that creates

a world

accepting rain

and punishment

the yellows

and oranges

the green time

the physical

some days

it's a blue world

a buzz of flies

somewhere music

this dance

of the actual

giving itself

to the eyes

a reflecting surface

designed

for survival

every glance

some circumference

of shadow

calling into

the psyche's

paper-blue

hieratic light

cardinals flaunt

their red into

a gentle rain

soft and constant

when elsewhere

becomes

an image

a thing

to live with

a worn feeling

an old force

softening glass

is there more

sadness in beauty

than beauty

in sadness

the fluorescent

afternoon sang

Romanticism

Why not consider the squirrel

in its leafy surround?

It may be in a state

of impersonal grief

for all I know.

Nature morphing

and dying and

looping all around it.

Something we share,

silence and time,

and we go on, blinking.

There will be stories

of an ancient kind.

Stories filled with forgetting

and paradox, with

trapdoors and mirrors.

An inflection of the real.

What is the real

but a reflecting pool

when I saw you once

ripple and wave.

All I see right now

is the world

playing air guitar

and I'm here now,

breathing.

This is what I know.

To dart is an intransitive verb

and moves freely.

A dart draws blood

when it's a noun.

Sure, you like it tough

but bruise easy.

Exquisite the veins

in a dragonfly's wings.

In truth I live

in a multiverse

but still want you.

In my mind

I am counting ribs

in alabaster light.

Yesterday I was holding

a gemstone key

but threw it into the sun

to make it impossible

to recognize god.

Yesterday I was not

a funhouse doll.

Today I am counting

squirrels in my yard.

Today I am in love

with a dead letter office at sunset.

Leaves, veins, ribs, sunsets,

all turning to letters.

These letters becoming

a love poem, why not?

Roxy Music

The old language reminds us of tradition; of nights, of tapers billowing by the window; of balmy and aromatic breezes; recalls historically, our girl asks for a poem; each week or so says, where is my poem, you don't write no more, sluggard; I say, I don't care, when I see you and we buckle and your shirt is on the chair and the room is blowsy, poetry don't matter; after, when I saw you in the mirror, I wrote: poetry died today.

Of the Air

She talked to me. Were lovely days. A superb summer. Had a right to it. My birds were wild birds. Were new. I tried to understand. Loveliest days. Speaking of a voice. To know it better. I understood. Not the report. Not what matters. Does this mean. House and midnight. The windows.

•

Speechlessness. Long stumbling earnestness. I have never been able. Will be different. The greater part. From now on. But I shall play. Perhaps not. To have been. Must have thought. Be able to tell. On a different theme. About a man a woman. A third about a thing.

•

April or little signs. Shall survive. I do not think. Will take place. I have had. What does ever. A little effort. Rushing things. I am less given. Still have my fits. Be on guard. Be sure crying. In a state. Spoil everything.

•

Atrocious life. Can I forgive. Am I content. Would be repaired. Then fall questions. They will be calm.

•

I am satisfied. I need nothing. Forgive nobody. Then the fires. I know where I am. This ancient night. The recent night. I longed to. Look around often. All well at first. Proud as punch. It did not occur.

•

All my life. I might draw. Now at hand. If all goes well. May plague me. The one thing. Will be there. About the thing. Then I shall. Still alive. My not having. Not to know. The old fog calls. Blind road what. Well-charted hopes. This is a mistake. It is a weakness. There it is then. Time that remains. Itself I suppose.

•

Things pushed on. Most above me. Weary face. The long spike. Best when all day. Built proper night. Breadth he said. Could not fail. From my poor box. I was not judged. Midnight. Little wind.

•

Indeed I could not. Would not. She is summer. I am gabber. I was one day. Possible like any. Either faster. There was one day. From might have been. Were lovely days. And summer. My birds. Had trusted some. Was missing some.

Ecstatic Joy and Its Variants

as surely as this is about seeing you dance naked

it is also about the sky and Mahler in the wan distance
heard by a child

as surely as the sadness never leaves and that music
heals the night with its deeps and neon

as surely as the glow of the radiator at 3 a.m.,
a line of inquiry, souvenirs, a signature for the sun

O bed of stray barrettes, discourse, and water
bed of laughter, hot takes, dried blood
bed of cedar bows, pinhole light, thing music

surely this is about water jetting from a spring,
a languid rafting with no particular destination

as the old arguments, humans, how they rhyme,
stutter, get lost

this is also about conversations with the dead,
the only honest definition of silence

surely you are not listening to the words I am singing

about the last day of my life, the gift of blood,
the perfect text

are not all the sounds on my lyre about you

like a seam through the sky, glitter, sometime youth,
surely this is about the one thing you do to me

places not even music has touched

and in my outrage, I am immortal
because I love, I am here

But the Heart in a Sense Is Far from Me Floating Out There

Hold on to the afterlife of the beloved, it's the only thing
    that's yours

Hold on to whatever magic in the backyard where we bury
    our thoughts, things of the world

Things of the world like an afterlife of the world to bury
    our setting outness

It's right to extract bone from the afterlife, dust collecting shoes,
    relics of the afterlife

Cut a hole in the poem to play peekaboo with the afterlife

Rebuild my house out of sky, blur my memoria into song

Make my headdress the right size to salute the emptiness
    alive in the beloved

The humanness of the beloved, the beloved and the night sky

Shapes floating out there becoming the beloved, the abstract,
   the total

Spooky Action

I want to use all the words tonight.

Words to open the backseat in the discourse.

Words to dilate and amplify the total disco night.

Forget daylight, I prefer a dark tenderness.

Prefer the sun at night when the discourse awakens

a quicksilver imago in the undertow.

I am using all the words now.

Tonight I am as the sky is, streaky.

The body falling away into a dusky word.

Quiet, intimate, sprung, exciting the sorceries in me.

To be unleashed as a verb.

Free to twirl, to disco, to walk away undone.

Consider the Wound

no ideas but in wounds, I is that wound

with its slight aura, archival glamour, gas-lit corridors,
its famous sunsets that dayglo on water

the storied rays travel

to consider wounds that grow through life, illuminate,
and expand into a primal struggle

to be able to say, I was here

an everyday annunciation the wound lifts from sorrow,
and it grows, taking years to love

a wound in all its glory

days go on watching clouds change into the mirror
of the world, which is my face

which is a threshold, a name, a proving ground,
an education in wounds

I can't explain it, I know it's true, like when a dove
becomes a scarf

this is what it feels like to come

the skyline bent in the window, autumnal consonants,
a musical light, it was good

the imagination fan-like shadows the garden reflecting
the primitive

a scent of camphor

days go on broadly scattered and move from a state
of unknowing

to a condition of the unknown

consider the wound with its canonical doubt, call stories
and testimony

indexical zeal for origins and etymologies

wund, wuntho, wunda, und

the mother opens every wound, the wound opens
every word

the asymmetries of a body in the act of elegy, ungainly
in its pilgrimage

trauma in the genes

a cellular memory of torn events

walking beneath a shadow of warplanes, shadows falling
on the wildflowers and timothy grass

days with their loud repetitive phrasing spiraling down
the scale, carry and echo

their uneven sky of development

and the magnificence of a backward glance, proud trees
and hillocks, proud lakes

the privileged nostalgia of that

or the podium in dead air and the sound of power, dead
air in which we wait for the candidates to enter

the sound of dead air and the dead metallurgical sound
of power

a static gunpowder sting folding space

to feel the wrought iron columns and buttresses rising
in the boy

welding the triumphal history of the industrial dawn
to the soft tissue of the body

a full bleed

who replaced my child with this ledger, this ledger
with a screed

the heart in the adult measures five inches in length,
three inches in width

the average weight varies from ten to twelve ounces

days go on, warbled notes, a jumble of fussing

even the first hours of agony are still new, ancient
wounds trickle fresh blood

will I still be standing, when nothing is more than
enough?

to be nowhere

I could live there, far from myself, along with the crescent,
free to shimmer

and outlive my sorrow

consider its eerie call and every shape of pain

wounds of the field, how they grow, they toil not,
neither do they spin

consider the flesh, its tendentious commentary,
its kin rituals

its shrill monotony like a sewing machine, days with
their glottal rattle and high trill

what was it you wanted? were you talking to me?

days whistle and tweet their spackled feelings

wounds that neither sow nor reap yet the air feeds them

if a wound could speak, what would it say?

the ride is a dream?

windmills and war and children, sleep and waking,
the grifting of time flies through everything

for every wound belonging to me as good belongs to you

days go on, a harsh croak, a low quacking

consider the wound, to refuse closure, to not let go,
to lose oneself

in a majesty

tears soften the heart, welcome them into the theater,
let the salt run down my face

it may be the last thing I see

days with their systems, the mirror staged

days gone into a heady blossom of joy and sorrow,
a complex ecology

a necessary weather of becoming

the world woke me at 6 a.m., outside a field, a hollow
and an oak, the morning star above

the wound woke me with its light, hold on to the last
things I see and can't explain, to know its truth

to have felt this as a boy

soloing inside, worrying the syntax between wound
and wounding, a carnal dance

alive in a dark theater, what I can say

retreats back into a wound wrung out into abstraction,
blah

I want new vistas, visions, earth in my mouth,
a collective breath, sweet noise of becoming

a kind of testimony

a disordered proof, a part of sex, more than sex, it was
time, the nature of time, I sensed happening

that death is happening

all that was left is where I am now

ACKNOWLEDGMENTS

Thanks to the many editors of the journals where these poems appeared: *Aphros*, *The Arts Fuse*, *The Brooklyn Rail*, *The Cambridge Literary Review* (UK), *Cero*, *Conjunctions*, *Fieldnotes* (UK), *Granta* (UK), *Harper's*, *New England Review*, *New York Review of Books*, *The Poetry Review* (UK), *3 Fold*, *Volt*, *Volume* (UK), and *The Yale Review*.

Thanks to Elaine Equi for selecting the poem "Revisionary" for *The Best American Poetry 2023*, Scribners: New York.

Many thanks to James Haug for the broadside of the poem "Roxy Music," Scram Press: Northampton; to James Meetze for the chapbook *In the Air* (with photographs by Richard Kraft), Manor House: Los Angeles; to Luke Roberts and Amy Tobin for the chapbook *Romanticism*, Distance No Object: London; and to Wolfram Swets for the chapbook *Consider the Wound*, Tungsten Press: Amsterdam.

The poem "Creeley Song" is composed primarily from the titles of books by Robert Creeley.

The title of the poem "Notre Musique" is after the film by Jean-Luc Godard.

And last but not least, I want to thank my good friends who read drafts, gave useful feedback, and supported me during the writing of this book.

PETER GIZZI is the author of several collections of poetry, most recently *Now It's Dark*, *Archeophonics*, *In Defense of Nothing*, and *Threshold Songs*, all from Wesleyan. In 2020 Carcanet brought out *Sky Burial: New and Selected Poems* in the UK.

His honors include the Lavan Younger Poet Award from the Academy of American Poets, and fellowships in poetry from The Rex Foundation, The Fund for Poetry, The Howard Foundation, The Foundation for Contemporary Arts, The John Simon Guggenheim Memorial Foundation, and the Judith E. Wilson Visiting Fellowship in Poetry at the University of Cambridge. In 2018 Wesleyan published *In the Air: Essays on the Poetry of Peter Gizzi*.

His editing projects have included *o·blēk: a journal of language arts*, *The Exact Change Yearbook*, *The House That Jack Built: The Collected Lectures of Jack Spicer*, and, with Kevin Killian, *My Vocabulary Did This to Me: The Collected Poetry of Jack Spicer*. From 2007 to 2012 he was the poetry editor for *The Nation*.

He teaches poetry and poetics in the MFA program at the University of Massachusetts, Amherst.

Library of Congress Cataloging-in-Publication Data

Names: Gizzi, Peter, author.

Title: Fierce elegy / Peter Gizzi.

Description: First edition. | Middletown, Connecticut : Wesleyan
    University Press, [2023] | Series: Wesleyan poetry | Summary:
    "Luminous and musical poems about love, time, and the intensity
    of the world as one turns to face the end of life" — Provided by
    publisher.

Identifiers: LCCN 2023008266 (print) | LCCN 2023008267 (ebook) |
    ISBN 9780819500670 (cloth) | ISBN 9780819500687 (paper) |
    ISBN 9780819500694 (e-book)

Subjects: BISAC: POETRY / Subjects & Themes / Death, Grief, Loss |
    LCGFT: Poetry.

Classification: LCC PS3557.I94 F54 2023 (print) | LCC PS3557.I94
    (ebook) | DDC 811/.54—dc23/eng/20230228

LC record available at https://lccn.loc.gov/2023008266

LC ebook record available at https://lccn.loc.gov/2023008267